The Ultimate Lady's Guide
TO BUYING A HOME

The Ultimate Lady's Guide
TO BUYING A HOME

SYLVIA M. BROUSSARD

Table of Contents

Defining Your Ideal Home

Many people contemplate the idea of home ownership for years and have no idea where to begin. They are under the misconception that to purchase a home, they must have at least 20% as a down payment and this is not always the case. As you walk through the following pages, you will gain a greater understanding of the entire home buying process, which begins with a few simple questions to help you identify what is most important to you in your new home.

Home means many different things to many different people. For some people, home means a gathering place for special life events. For others, it could be a place of refuge to relax and unwind from a demanding business and hectic travel schedule. The first thing you need to consider is what does home mean to you.

Buying a home is much more than purchasing a house; you must consider your family structure, your work arrangements, and your lifestyle. Another important factor that often gets overlooked are the dislikes of the previous residence and neighborhood. It is useless to find what seems to be the ideal home if it is an hour or so away from all the activities you and your family participate in several times a week.

Many families are multi-generational, so you should start by determining who will be living in your home? Will you have family members, like aging parents that you will need special accommodations for, or family members that visit you on a regular basis for more than a few days at a time?

Now, let us discuss what your work life will look like. If there are family members who will be working outside of your home, you must decide what would be a comfortable commute in time and/or distance. If someone will be working from home, what tools, equipment or systems will they need in the home to operate effectively and efficiently?

One of the most important considerations, yet sometimes overlooked, are lifestyle factors. It is imperative to the success of finding the ideal home to have a discussion with all family members that will be living in the home to find out what their most important activities are. Some of the more common examples of lifestyle factors to be considered are schools, recreational activities, religious institutes, cultural activities, entertainment, sports, shopping, restaurants and hobbies. What will you add to your list?

____

____

____

____

Now let's focus a bit more on the neighborhood and the home itself. We are familiar with the common questions of how many bedrooms, bathrooms, and garages, but you should think a little outside of the box. What are a few of your favorite features you liked most about your previous residence? What are some of the things you wish you could have in your new home? You may include a particular floor plan that you prefer because it has an open kitchen and the master bedroom is located at the rear of the home. You may want a small yard so that you can maintain it yourself, or you may want to live in a certain neighborhood because you have friends or family members that live there.

____

____

____

____

____

As stated earlier, one of the most often overlooked factors in defining your ideal home are the things you disliked most about your previous home or neighborhood. It is equally important to identify the things you dislike as well as the things you like. Many home buyers are so caught up in what they want in a home, that they never notice the things that they don't want in a home or neighborhood. Please take a moment to list anything that you disliked about your previous dwelling or neighborhood. Be mindful to avoid these items when you are in the process of searching for your new home?

____

____

____

____

____

Finally, we get to discuss the topic that everyone usually wants to discuss, but we will take it a little deeper. These are the features and/or amenities that the home or neighborhood must have in them in order for you to make a purchase. This is more than just the features that you and your family desire, but they are essential to the everyday life of your family.

One example would be that a bedroom downstairs with a private shower would be considered a "must have" if you were taking care of an aging parent who could not climb up and down the stairs. Another example could be having a gas range instead of an electric one for the gourmet chef who only cooks with an open flame. Now it's your turn to list your "must haves" in the spaces below. Take some time and really give this some thought, as you could potentially be in this home for the next 30 years or more. Why are these items important to you and your family?

____

____

____

Assessing Your Needs

Selecting and purchasing the right home is an extremely personalized process, that begins with identifying your family's needs.

As you think about finding your ideal home, the following pages will assist you in clarifying your needs. Some of the areas that will be explored are:

- The priorities, values, and interests you want this move to support.
- The features you are looking for in a home.
- Analyzing a neighborhood to determine if it matches your lifestyle.
- Creating a tailored approach to your home search that fits your plans.
- Setting expectations between all parties involved throughout the home buying process.

The Ultimate Lady's Notes

Preparation for the Home Finding Process

This section will aid in simplifying the home search and buying process to make it an enjoyable experience for you. Because many people only buy homes once in their lifetime, or at most, once every seven years or so, it is recommended that you seek out and obtain a real estate professional that is knowledgeable in the area that you are interested in living. You will want to consider the following information and have it prepared to share with the real estate professional, or have them assist you with it if you are unsure about anything.

Where are you in the home finding process? Are you just thinking about the possibility of buying a home, or committed to making a move? How long have you been looking for a home? The real estate professional may want to know if you have been searching on your own, or if you have contacted any other real estate professionals. List where you are in the process to evaluate.

____

____

Why are you considering the purchase of a home at this time?

____

____

When are you wanting to be in your home? Is there a specific date that you must be settled in your new home?

____

____

Are there any other individuals that will be included in the decision-making of this home purchase? If so, they should be brought into the process at the very beginning.

____

____

Have you ever purchased a home or any other type of real estate before? If so, when was the last transaction completed? Things change so rapidly and sporadically in different markets that you may be surprised at some of the current requirements that have been included since your last purchase.

____

If you have purchased a home in the past, list what you enjoyed most about that experience? If you have never bought a home, what do you think will be most exciting about the experience?

____

____

Were there any unpleasant experiences in your previous home finding journey that you hope to avoid? If this is your first home purchase, are there any problems or concerns that you may have?

____

____

Will you be paying cash for your new home or are you planning to finance it? Are you aware of your financing options? There are additional options available to potential homeowners that require much less than a 20% down payment and you don't have to a 30-year mortgage!

____

____

Have you ever worked with a real estate professional before? If so, what did you like about that experience? Are there any expectations that you would like to see repeated with your new real estate professional? Please be specific about the minimum services and support you expect. Your real estate professional may have certain expectations as well and they should be communicated at the onset of the relationship. Experience has proven that conflict only arises when expectations differ.

____

____

____

The Process of Purchasing a Home

The process of purchasing a home typically includes many of the following elements. Allow your real estate professional to be your resource and guide through the entire process.

Initial Consultation

- Determine your priorities and needs
- Review "agency" choices and select appropriate working relationship
- Discuss financing options

Finding the Right Home

- Sales associate to show you properties based on your criteria
- Evaluate each property with sales associate
- Choose the right home

Obtain Financing

- Find a mortgage company
- Consult with a loan officer
- Pre-qualification
- Complete Loan Application
- Obtain loan pre-approval
- Provide requested documentation
- Property appraisal
- Loan Processing
- Final loan approval

Preparing an Offer
- Review comparable sales to determine offer price
- Review progress of loan pre-approval; decide on financing
- Decide on other terms (inspections, possession date, personal property, etc.)
- Prepare earnest money deposit

Reaching an Agreement with a Seller
- Present your offer
- Negotiation of terms and possible counteroffers
- Agree upon sales contract with seller

Completing the Settlement Process
- Deposit of earnest money
- Review seller's property disclosures
- Review preliminary title report
- Roof, termite, and other inspections
- Remove any remaining contingencies
- Arrange for home owner's insurance
- Arrange for home warranty
- Arrange for movers
- Final walk-through of property with sales associate
- Provide balance of down payment and closing costs
- Sign Documents
- Loan Funding
- Recording of Title
- Receive keys from sales associate

Move In!

Financing Your Home

Many buyers are unable to purchase a home with all cash so obtaining a home loan, also known as a mortgage, is necessary to complete the purchase. Your real estate professional should be able to assist you with finding a residential lender to ensure that you obtain the financing that meets your needs.

It is recommended that you get pre-approved for a loan prior to beginning your home search. This allows you to know your purchasing power and it will guide the real estate professional to only search for properties within the approved budget. Getting pre-approved for a loan also gives you a stronger negotiating position when submitting an offer on a home and it saves time in the final loan approval process.

Your real estate professional should be able to put you in contact with a few experienced loan officers at reputable mortgage companies. Your loan officer will be your principal guide through the financing process. They will discuss the various types of financing options may be currently available to you, including:

- o   Conventional Fixed-Rate Mortgage
- o   Adjustable Rate Mortgage (ARM)
- o   Government-assisted (FHA, VA, or USDA) financing
- o   Seller-assisted financing

The lender will be asking you for personal information regarding your income, expenses and other financial obligations to establish your credit worthiness. I have included a generic loan application list to guide you in the collection of items that may be needed to process your loan. You may not need all of the items on the list, however it is always a good rule of thumb to have them readily available.

Loan Application Checklist

The following is simply a guide for the information a loan officer may request when you apply for a mortgage.

Purchase contract and property information

- ☐ Copy of the sales contract
- ☐ Mailing address and property description
- ☐ Contact information for access to the property
- ☐ Plans and specifications (new construction only)

Personal information

- ☐ Social Security number
- ☐ Age
- ☐ Years of schooling
- ☐ Marital status
- ☐ Number and ages of dependents
- ☐ Current address and telephone number
- ☐ Addresses for the past seven years
- ☐ Current housing expenses (rent, mortgage, insurance, taxes)
- ☐ Name and address of landlord or mortgage holder for the past two years

Employment history and income

- ☐ Two years of employment history, with complete details of each job
- ☐ Recent pay stubs and two years of W-2 forms
- ☐ Complete tax returns and financial statements if self-employed
- ☐ A written explanation of employment gaps
- ☐ Records of dividends and interest received
- ☐ Proof of other income

Assets

- ☐ Complete information on all bank and money market accounts
- ☐ Two months of bank statements
- ☐ The current value of stocks, bonds, mutual funds, and other investments
- ☐ Vested interest in retirement funds
- ☐ Value of life insurance
- ☐ Information on the vehicle you own
- ☐ Information on real estate you own
- ☐ Value of significant personal property you own

Liabilities

- ☐ Itemized list of all current debts (loans, credit cards, and other bills)
- ☐ A written explanation of past credit problems
- ☐ Full details of bankruptcy during the last seven years

Fees

- ☐ Credit report and appraisal fees (usually $500 or less)

Your Personal Source for Property Information

We have access to virtually every home for sale in this market and we are able to show you the ones that best align with your requirements, including:

- All homes marketed by Broussard Fine Homes Group
- All properties listed by brokers through the Multiple Listing Service (MLS)
- Properties not necessarily on the open market
- Many properties offered "For Sale by Owner"

To save time, hassle and duplicated effort, call us for additional information on properties you see, whether or not they are being offered by a Broussard Fine Homes Group sales professional. We can obtain important facts about:

- Advertisements in newspapers or buyer's guides
- Listings on the internet
- Open Houses
- Houses displaying any "For Sale" Sign

The Ultimate Lady's Notes

Looking for Your Ideal Home

Discovering the right home is an exciting event. As a Broussard Fine Homes Group real estate professional, our commitment is to make your home search as stress-free and efficient as possible.

- We will schedule a home buyer orientation to identify your budget to save time and frustration in the home finding process. We will then consider your financing options and begin the mortgage pre-approval process as soon as possible.

- Next, we will select only the properties that most closely meet your unique needs, interests, lifestyle and budget, and send you a list to drive by to see if you like the neighborhood and the curb appeal of the home. It is best to preview only a few homes at a time, at different times of the day that may be of interest to you.

- Once you narrow the list down, we will schedule a time to look at the interior of your top three homes and neighborhoods. The appointments are scheduled with the sellers through a showing service or their real estate broker's office.

- If the seller or their real estate professional is at the property when we visit, it would be best for you to limit your conversation with them, as anything you say may be used against you during the negotiation process.

- Many homes are equipped with electronic recording devices, so it is best to use the Home Finding Worksheet that is included in this book or an electronic or physical notebook to take notes of your thoughts and evaluation of each home during our visits to the homes. We will discuss the home once we leave the property.

- To enable us in identifying your ideal home, we will ask you to tell us your thoughts about each property you see, both positive and negative. If no home excites you enough to submit an offer, we will re-assess your needs and buying criteria.

Home Finding Worksheet

Evaluation of (property address):

____

Size (number of rooms or square footage):

____

HOA Dues $ _______   Asking Price $_________

Date Visited _____________

Most Memorable Feature:

____

INTERIOR

Overall Condition

____

Floor Plan

____

Bedrooms/Baths

Living Room

Family Room

Dining Room

Kitchen/Laundry

Heating/Air

Other Features

EXTERIOR

Overall Condition

Paint and Trim

Roof

Deck/Patio/Pool

Garage

Landscape/fence

Other Features

LOCATION

Appearance of neighborhood

____

House value relative to area

____

Distance to employment, schools, shopping, etc.

____

SUMMARY

Favorite Features

____

Least desirable features

____

Comments

____

Examining the Costs

It is helpful to have an estimate of the costs associated with purchasing a home.

Costs Required to Close the Transaction:

Title Insurance	$______
Settlement Fees	$______
Recording Fees	$______
Property Tax (pro-rated)	$______
Loan Origination Fee	$______
Appraisal	$______
Credit Report	$______
Other Loan Fees	$______
Interest on New Loan (pro-rated)	$______
Home Warranty	$______
Termite Inspection	$______
Other Inspections (roof, property, geological, etc.)	$______
Homeowner's Insurance	$______
Total Estimated Closing Costs	$______

Estimated Monthly Payment:

Principal and Interest	$______
Property Tax	$______
Homeowner's Insurance	$______
Private Mortgage Insurance (PMI)	$______
Homeowner's Association Dues	$______

Home Purchase Summary:

Purchase Price of Home $__________

Down Payment $__________

Amount Financed $__________

Estimated Closing Costs $__________

Estimated Monthly Payment $__________

***This is a preliminary estimate only. Actual costs will vary depending on the property, the lender and other factors. You will receive a detailed breakdown of costs before the closing of the transaction from your lender.**

Determining Affordability

It is a wise practice to assess your finances before starting the home buying process.

Step 1
Monthly Income

Wages, salary, business income after expenses $______
Interest, dividends, or rental income $______
Other Income
(alimony, child support, retirement) $______
Total Monthly Income $______

Step 2
Monthly Non-Housing Expenses

Food/Clothing $______
Medical (include premiums and prescriptions) $______
Life Insurance $______
Child Care $______
Automobile (loan, insurance, maintenance) $______
Education/Student Loans $______
Travel/Recreation $______
Credit Card Payments $______
Bank Loan Payments (other than mortgage) $______
Alimony or Child Support Owed $______
Savings and Investments $______
Income Taxes $______
Total Monthly Non-Housing Expenses $______

Step 3
Amount Available for Monthly Housing Expenses

Total Monthly Income (Step 1) $______
Minus Total Non-Housing Expenses (Step 2) $______

= Amount Available for
Monthly Housing Expenses $______

Step 4
Monthly Estimated House Expenses

Mortgage Loan Payment (principal + interest) $______
Property Taxes $______
Mortgage Insurance $______
Homeowner's Insurance (liability, floor, fire) $______
Utilities (heat, water, electricity, gas, trash) $______
Maintenance and Repairs $______
Other (assessments, association dues) $______
Total Monthly Estimated
Housing Expenses (Step 3). $______

Compare Step 3 and Step 4 totals. The Total Monthly Estimated Housing Expenses (Step 4) should not exceed the amount available for Monthly Housing Expenses (Step 3).

Submitting Your Offer

Once you have found your ideal property, the next step in the process is to submit an offer to purchase the home. You will consult with your real estate professional to determine the price you want to offer, your desired closing date, any personal items that you would like included with the sale of the home, and any warranties, home inspections, or repairs that you would like the completed prior to closing. This information will be included in your initial offer.

The seller's asking price may or may not be realistic, so your real estate professional should complete a Comparative Market Analysis, also known as a CMA, to determine the current market value. The CMA analyzes properties that are similar to your selected property that have recently been sold, gone into a pending status, are actively listed on the market, and those that have failed to be sold. You will then examine the costs that will be associated with purchasing the home you selected and choose the price you want to offer.

Your real estate professional will submit the offer you have decided upon. The seller will either accept your offer as it is presented, reject it completely, or propose that adjustments be made to your offer and resubmitted. This is called a counteroffer. If there is a counteroffer, you can choose to accept it, reject it or counter it. This may continue until we have an offer acceptable to both the buyer and the seller. Once you have reached an agreement with the seller and the contract is signed and dated by both parties, you have an executed contract to purchase the home.

When the contract has been submitted, we will work with the loan officer to explain which financing options are available, including the current interest rates and terms of the available loan options. Then you will need to decide which mortgage best fits your financial requirements and submit any additional paperwork required by the loan officer to process the loan.

Protecting Your Interests

There are many ways to help you protect your interests in the purchase of a home. Listed here are a few of the most common ones:

- A **written property disclosure statement** from the seller will be provided to you to reveal any problems with the home and the surrounding area that they are aware of.

- **Professional inspections** can reveal structural, roof, termite, and other problems with the property that the seller will need to remedy prior to closing.

- A **home warranty** can give you peace of mind by providing repair-or-replacement coverage of major home operating systems and appliances.

- A **walk-through** before closing will allow you to make sure all required work has been completed and the property is ready to become yours.

The Ultimate Lady's Notes

After Your Offer Is Accepted

Many details need to be taken care of for a home purchase to be completed. It can take 15-60 days to complete all the steps involved in a home sale, depending on the complexity of the transactions. Your real estate professional should work closely with everyone involved to help ensure that the transaction moves ahead as smoothly as possible. They should explain in detail each step that will occur and answer any questions you might have.

You will learn about option periods, earnest money, surveys, and title commitments, to name a few things. Your real estate professional will spend time communicating with the seller's broker to make sure that the seller fulfills their responsibilities under the contract. They should stay in touch with the settlement officer, title officer, lender and others to help coordinate their activities and to help keep the transaction moving forward.

During this time, they should communicate with you on a regular basis to guide you and ensure that you are as informed as possible.

Your Guide to a Smooth Transition

Here is a simple guide of items that you should be mindful of during the four weeks prior to moving to your new home. Your real estate professional should be able to suggest local professionals for many of these services. Place this list on your refrigerator so that you can be reminded daily of items that need to be completed prior to your move.

4 weeks before you move

- ☐ Set up your move with a reputable moving company.
- ☐ Arrange for school records to be transferred.
- ☐ Arrange to transfer or take with you all medical, dental and other important records.
- ☐ Prepare to transfer your homeowner's and auto insurance to ensure that you will be covered for any unforeseeable disasters.
- ☐ Keep track of moving-related expenses. (Check with your accountant to find out what expenses will be deductible).

3 weeks before you move

- ☐ Complete change-of-address requests for the post office, subscriptions, credit card companies, and important contacts.

2 weeks before you move

- ☐ Arrange for final utility reading at your former residence the day after your move.
- ☐ Have utilities and phone turned on at your new home the day before you move in.
- ☐ Close or transfer bank accounts.
- ☐ Terminate home delivery service.
- ☐ Arrange for transfer of vehicle and driver's licenses.
- ☐ Have an extra supply of prescription medications for the next four weeks.

The week of your move

- ☐ We will schedule a final walk-through of the property to make sure everything is in order.
- ☐ Keep valuable financial records and personal papers with you; do not pack them with the rest of your household goods.
- ☐ On closing day, the home purchase documents are recorded, the loan is funded, and the home is yours.
- ☐ Move in!

After you move in

- ☐ Consider plans for landscaping design, installation, and maintenance.
- ☐ Review home security requirements and systems.
- ☐ New home furnishings, appliances, and interior decorating will help you make the house your home.

Enjoy your new home!

The Ultimate Lady's Notes

The Ultimate Lady's Notes

The Ultimate Lady's Notes

The Ultimate Lady's Notes

Sylvia M. Broussard is a native Texan who takes pride in being the consummate real estate professional. Since the inception of her real estate career in 2000, she has gained a vast amount of experience in various types of real estate transactions in the U.S. and abroad, which has earned her recognition as an invaluable resource to her domestic and global clientele of residential and commercial real estate buyers, sellers, and investors.

Sylvia is highly respected for her expertise, integrity, hard work, negotiation and problem-solving skills, as well as her determination to get the job done on time while exceeding the expectations of her clients. As a Real Estate Broker, she is committed to helping each client accomplish their real estate goals.

Prior to starting her real estate career, Sylvia traveled the globe as the wife of a now-retired United States Marine. During this tenure, she gained extensive experience and became meticulous in the specialized area of representing relocating professionals and service members. She understands first-hand the needs of relocating families.